Amphibians of North America
Frogs, Toads, Salamanders

Billy Grinslott & Kinsey Marie Books

ISBN - 9781965098547

Spadefoot toads live in many parts of the USA, including the East Coast, the Southwest, and the West. Spadefoot toads prefer sandy or loose soils that are easy to dig into, or small bodies of water. They spend most of their time underground but come out at night to feed. The name spadefoot comes from the spade-shaped tubercle on their hind feet that helps them dig. Spadefoot tadpoles can hatch in as little as 24 hours and can grow into land-dwelling amphibians in as little as 14 days. Spadefoots can produce skin secretions that are poisonous or unpalatable to a predator. When injured or handled roughly, spadefoots give off a smell like roasted peanuts or garlic.

Yosemite toads live in the Sierra Nevada mountains of California. They can be found at elevations up to 12,000 ft. Yosemite toads live in rivers, streams, temporary pools and can be found in meadows, where adult males make small holes to call from. They spend most of their time in underground burrows to keep cool and hide from predators. Yosemite toads walk instead of hopping and can walk up to a mile between burrows. As tadpoles, Yosemite toads eat algae and other plant materials. As adults, they eat invertebrates like ants, flies, beetles, and spiders.

Narrow-mouthed toads live in the southeastern and lower midwestern regions of the USA. The two species of narrow-mouthed toads are the Eastern and the Western Narrow-mouthed Toads. Narrow-mouthed toads are mostly ant eaters. They have a skin fold behind their eyes that protects them from ant bites while feeding. They are solitary and spend most of their time in burrows or under rocks or logs. Males produce a loud, high-pitched bleating call. They can secrete a noxious substance on their skin that can irritate predators. They are one of the smallest toads in North America, usually only reaching around an inch in length.

Western toads live in the western USA, parts of Canada, and Alaska. They are found in mountain ranges and higher elevations, from the Rocky Mountains to the Pacific Coast. Western toads can grow to be five inches long. Like all toads, they have warts on their skin. Western toads have a chirping, duck-like call. Western toads secrete a foul-tasting liquid from the glands on their back and behind their eyes to defend themselves from predators. Tadpoles eat aquatic plants, while adults eat algae, insects, worms, and other small insects. Western toads may spend up to seven months of the year in hibernation during cold months.

American toads live in the eastern USA and Canada. American toads live in a variety of habitats. They are commonly found in backyards. American toads are nocturnal, and they can eat up to 1,000 insects per day. American toads have sticky tongues that they use to catch prey. American toads have glands on the back of their heads that produce a poisonous secretion called bufotoxin. This secretion can be fatal to small animals and cause allergic reactions in humans.

Cane toads are found in Florida, Hawaii, and Texas in the United States. They are also found in the Caribbean Islands, Guam, Puerto Rico, and other US territories. Cane toads can live in a variety of habitats. Cane toads eat almost anything, including animals. Cane toads secrete poison from the glands behind their shoulders. This poison can kill animals that bite or eat them, including pets. Dogs are especially prone to be poisoned by licking or biting toads. Cane toads toxic poison can irritate human skin and burn the eyes.

Gopher frogs use burrows for shelter, that's how they got their name. Gopher frogs are found in the southeastern USA. Gopher frogs come in many shades of green, and they have speckles that help them hide in vegetation. Gopher frog tadpoles can be yellow-green, olive-green, or gray with black spots. Gopher frogs eat a variety of insects. Male gopher frogs make calls that sound like snoring. When threatened, gopher frogs shield their eyes with their hands. Gopher frogs are covered in warts that secrete a milky substance. They can grow to be over four inches long.

Leopard frogs live in many parts of the USA. Leopard frogs are typically brown or green with dark spots on their backs and legs. Leopard frogs make a croak or call that is a long snoring sound followed by a series of croaks, grunts, or chuckles. They can grow to be 4.5 inches long. Tadpole leopard frogs have eyes on top of their heads, unlike other frog species. Leopard frogs can jump up to 6 feet. Leopard frogs hibernate in the winter at the bottom of ponds or streams, buried in sediment or under rocks or logs.

Rain frogs are known for their defensive squeaking sound and their ability to puff themselves up to appear bigger and more intimidating. Rain frogs can puff up like a balloon to appear more intimidating. Rain frogs can grow to 3 inches long. Rain frogs are native to southern Africa, but some have been released in the USA. Rain frogs have flat, spade-shaped feet that help them dig. Rain frogs lay eggs in shallow underground nests, and the eggs hatch into froglets instead of tadpoles.

American bullfrogs are native to the eastern and central USA. Bullfrogs prefer warm, slow, or stagnant waters with lots of vegetation. American bullfrogs are the largest frog in North America, growing up to 8 inches long and weighing up to 1 pound. They are carnivorous and eat a wide variety of animals, including crayfish, fish, snails, birds, and other frogs. Only male bullfrogs croak, making a sound like jug-o-rum. They croak to attract mates and establish territory. Bullfrogs can jump distances 10 times their body length, up to 6 feet.

Pig frogs get their name from the grunting sound they make, that sounds like a pig grunting. Pig frogs are typically 3 to 6 inches long, with a maximum length of 6.5 inches. Pig frogs live in the southeastern coastal plains of the USA, Pig frogs live in permanent bodies of water, such as ponds, lakes, and marshes. Pig frogs eat crayfish, dragonflies, beetles, and other aquatic invertebrates. Pig frogs move by hopping, leaping, and swimming. Pig frogs burrow into mud at the bottom of ponds or wetlands to hibernate during the winter. Pig frogs have webbing to the tips of their hind feet, to help them swim.

Pickerel frogs are medium-sized frogs that are usually 2 to 4 inches long. Pickerel frogs have two rows of large, dark spots on their back. Pickerel frogs live in the eastern and midwestern USA. Pickerel frogs are the only poisonous frog's native to the USA. Their skin secretions can irritate humans and are fatal to many small animals. Many snakes and mammals avoid pickerel frogs because of their toxic skin secretions. Pickerel frogs make a low nasal snore, like a mooing of a cow. Pickerel frog tadpoles take around three months to turn into frogs.

Cricket frogs are named for their call, which sounds like two pebbles tapping together. Cricket frogs are small frogs that are usually less than 1.5 inches long. Cricket frogs live in many areas of the USA. Cricket frogs live around freshwater habitats, such as ponds, lakes, streams, and rivers. They prefer sunny, shallow water with lots of vegetation. The cricket frog is one of the best jumping amphibians, able to jump more than 60 times its body length. Some species of cricket frogs include the northern, the eastern, and the Blanchard's cricket frog

Cascades frogs grow to about three inches long. Cascades frogs are often found in the Cascade and Olympic Mountains of Washington, Oregon, and California. They have small bumps on their backs and sides, and their eyes are positioned to the sides. The colors on their backs can change to attract other frogs. They are diurnal, meaning they are active during the day. They are also known to bask on the sun on water-covered rocks. Cascades frogs hibernate during the winter by burrowing into the muddy bottoms of lakes and ponds. Their calls can be low-pitched, grating, and chuckling, or a series of rapid clucks.

American water frogs grow up to 6 inches long. They have Green or olive front skin with darker colors on their back. American water frogs have streamlined bodies and webbed feet that help them swim. American water frogs are known for their vocalizations, which include croaks, trills, and peeps. They use these sounds to communicate with other frogs. Frogs have excellent night vision and are sensitive to movement. Male frogs have vocal sacs, which are pouches of skin that fill with air.

Tree frogs vary in size but are generally small and slender compared to other frogs. They live in many parts of the USA. There are several types of tree frogs. Tree frogs are known for their ability to climb trees, that's how they got their name. Tree frogs have adhesive toe pads that help them climb trees and other surfaces. Many tree frog species have vibrant colors. Tree frogs can change color to camouflage themselves. They also have long legs to help them jump. Tree frogs can breathe through their skin. Tree frogs can make sounds that can be heard from a mile away.

Chorus frogs are small and are usually less than 1.5 inches long. Chorus frogs live in many parts of the USA. Chorus frogs can survive freezing temperatures because they can increase their blood glucose levels, which acts as an antifreeze. Male chorus frogs can inflate their vocal sacs to make sounds that can be heard up to half a mile away. Chorus frogs can change color to match their surroundings. Chorus frogs have small toe pads that help them climb trees. Chorus frogs are thought to have evolved 200 million years ago.

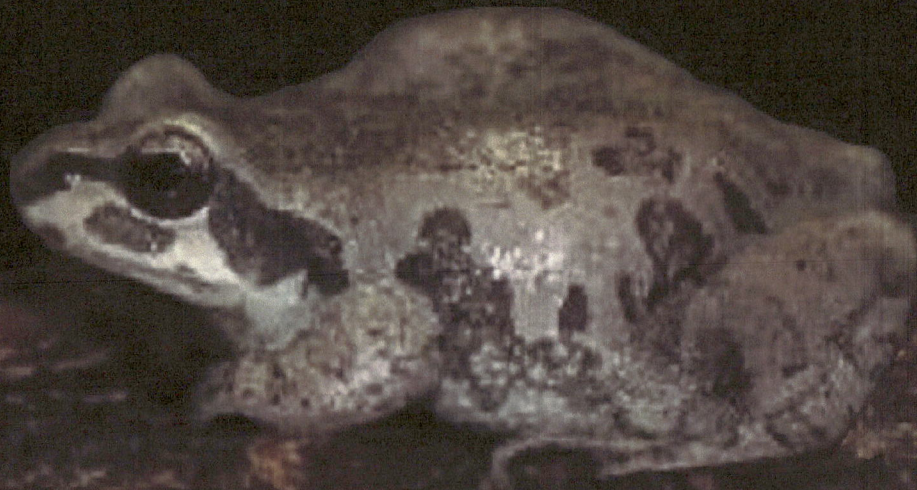

Wood frogs live in the northeastern United States, including the Upper Midwest, and in the forests of Alaska. Wood frogs are usually three inches long. Wood frogs can survive in freezing temperatures. Wood frogs can freeze and thaw without dying because their bodies use glucose and urea for protection. Wood frogs survive the winter by partially freezing. During this time, their hearts stop beating and they stop breathing. As it warms up, they thaw out and become active again. Wood frogs have glands that secrete a mild toxin onto their skin, but they are not a threat to humans.

Spotted frogs got their name because they have darker spots on their skin. The color of spotted frogs can change with age. They have a bumpy skin texture and are tan to dark olive in color with dark spots that often have light centers. Spotted frogs, including the Columbia spotted frog and the Oregon spotted frog, live in the western USA, from Alaska to California. They grow from 2 to 4 inches long. Female spotted frogs are usually larger than males. They can migrate long distances to find new water sources when their water sources dry up. They have long, sticky tongues that they use to catch and eat insects.

Mink frogs grow to be about 3 inches long. Mink frogs live in the northern USA and Canada. Mink frogs are primarily aquatic and live in cool, slow-moving bodies of water. They are rarely found away from water and only leave at night during rain. They make a rapid cut, cut, cut sound resembling a hammer striking wood. When mink frogs call in chorus it sounds like Horses hooves on a cobblestone road. When handled, they emit a strong rotten onion smelling odor. Tadpoles take about a year before turning into froglets. Mink frogs hibernate in the mud at the bottom of the lake to avoid freezing.

Red-legged frogs can grow up to 5.5 inches long. Red-legged frogs live in California, British Columbia and Mexico. The California red-legged is the largest native frog in the western USA. They live in or near still bodies of water, like ponds, lakes, and marshes. Red-legged frogs are nocturnal, they come out at night and eat insects, small mice, and fish. Most frogs cannot make sounds underwater, but the male red-legged frog can call from underwater or beneath ice. Red-legged frog tadpoles are herbivores that eat plants.

Spring peeper frogs live in the eastern USA and north into southern Canada. Spring peepers are small frogs that are usually 1.5 inches long. Spring peepers have vocal sacs that inflate like balloons to create their high-pitched peeping sounds. Spring peepers can be heard from a mile away. Spring peepers are good climbers due to their large toe pads. Thet Prefer to live in waters without fish. Spring peepers are nocturnal and well-camouflaged. They are more likely to be heard than seen.

Red-backed salamanders are small salamanders, measuring 2 to 4 inches long. Red-backed salamanders live in the eastern United States. Red-backed salamanders can drop their tail to escape predators. They will grow a new tail, but it may be a different color. Red-backed salamanders can recognize close relatives and sometimes take in young relatives during dry seasons. Red-backed salamanders have long tails that store fat and nutrients.

Tiger salamanders can grow to be 7 to 14 inches long, with the average size being around 7 to 8 inches. Tiger salamanders live in many parts of the USA. Tiger salamanders are nocturnal feeders that emerge from their burrows at night. They have specialized foot pads for digging. Tiger salamanders have semi-permeable skin that produces mucus to help them absorb moisture. Tiger salamanders can regenerate entire limbs, but the regenerated parts usually lack color. Tiger salamanders have a tail gland that produces a toxic, milky secretion for self-defense.

Olympic torrent salamanders are small salamanders that are less than 4 inches long, Olympic torrent salamanders live in the Pacific Northwest of the USA. They like to live in clear, cold, mountain streams. They are medium to dark brown with bright yellow undersides. They have small lungs and breathe mainly through their thin skin. They can regenerate lost limbs. When threatened, they roll over to show their yellow undersides. Olympic torrent salamanders have short snouts and large prominent eyes. They lay eggs in the water, and it takes their eggs about 1 year to hatch. The larvae can take more than two years to develop into a salamander.

Ensatina salamanders are are typically 4 inches long. They have short bodies and legs, and large eyes. There are many subspecies of Ensatina salamanders, including the Oregon, the Monterey, and the large-blotched Ensatina. They live along the west coast of North America, from Baja California to British Columbia. Ensatinas are lungless salamanders that breathe through their skin and the lining of their mouths. This makes them sensitive to changes in humidity and temperature. Ensatinas retreat underground to hide during hot and dry periods. Ensatinas have a detachable tail that they can drop to escape predators. Ensatinas can secrete a toxic, milky white substance from their tail to repel predators.

Spotted salamanders can grow to be 6 to 10 inches long. Spotted salamanders live in the eastern and southeastern USA, as well as southeastern Canada. Spotted salamanders live in damp, hidden environments, such as under rocks, logs, and leaf litter. Spotted salamanders have irregular rows of yellow or orange spots down their backs and tails. Spotted salamanders have several defense mechanisms. They can produce a bad-tasting toxin from glands on their backs and tails. They can detach their tail and regrow it if attacked. Their bright spots warn predators that they are toxic. Spotted salamanders can regrow legs, tails, organs, heads, or even parts of their brains.

Adult Klamath black salamanders can grow to be up to five inches long. Klamath black salamanders live in northern California and southern Oregon, in the Klamath Mountains. They are fully black with some bronze or green specks on their heads, backs, tails, and legs. They have a large, flat head with a broad, rounded snout. They have legs that are shorter than most salamanders. They have large eyes that don't protrude. Their tails are long, making up 90 percent of their total length Klamath black salamanders are lungless and breathe through their skin. Adults forage for small insects and invertebrates on the ground at night during wet weather.

Red-spotted newts can grow to be 5 inches long. Red-spotted newts live in the eastern and central USA, and Canada. Red-spotted newts have bright red or orange colors with spots. This coloration warns predators that the newt is toxic. Their toxins are lethal to most predators, but some snakes, are immune. Red-spotted newts have three life stages: larvae, efts, and adults. Larvae live in water, efts live on land, and adults live in water again. They help to control mosquito populations by eating mosquito larvae.

Jefferson salamanders can grow up to 7 inches long. Jefferson salamanders live in northeastern USA. They spend most of the year underground, Jefferson salamanders are long and slender with a broad snout and long toes. They may have blue flecks on their limbs and lower body. Jefferson salamanders can live up to 30 years, which is much longer than most amphibians. Jefferson salamanders are carnivorous, eating worms, insects, and other small invertebrates. Predators of Jefferson salamanders include raccoons, shrews, and skunks.

Marbled salamanders can grow to 4.5 inches long. They are stout-bodied salamanders with a black body and light-colored crossbars or bands on their back, tail and head. Marbled salamanders live in the eastern United States. They are most found in damp forests, woodlands, and areas with wet soil. Marbled salamanders are active at night and hide under logs and vegetation during the day. They burrow deep into the soil to survive dry periods. Marbled salamanders have poison glands in their tails. Marbled salamanders are considered a keystone predator because they alter the competitive ability of their prey.

Long-tailed salamanders can grow to 8 inches long. Their tails are two-thirds of their total length. Long-tailed salamanders live in the eastern USA. Long-tailed salamanders are typically yellow, but can also be red, orange, or brown. Long-tailed salamanders communicate using pheromones, which are chemical smells. Kind of like perfume for humans. Salamanders can regenerate lost limbs, including tails and toes, within a few weeks.

Mole salamanders can grow to 5 inches long. Mole salamanders live in the eastern and central USA. They can be light gray, light brown, dark gray, or black, with light gray flecks on their backs and sides. Their heads and feet are large compared to the rest of their bodies. They spend most of their time underground or under objects like logs and rocks. Mole salamanders are carnivores that eat worms, mollusks, arthropods, and crayfish. When threatened, mole salamanders may lash their tails, head-butt, bite, twist around, flee, or pretend to be dead. Mole salamanders are territorial and will defend their area.

Green salamanders can grow to 5 inches long. Green salamanders live in the Appalachian Mountains area and can be found in the eastern and midwestern USA. Green salamanders have flattened out bodies and long legs. Their flat bodies help them squeeze into tight spaces on cliffs. They prefer shaded rock faces with crevices that provide cool temperatures. They have square-tipped toes and long rounded tails. Their bodies are covered with greenish markings. They don't have an aquatic larval life stage. Females lay their eggs in moist crevices in rocks. They are usually active at night due to the cooler and wetter conditions produced by mountain fog and evening dew. They don't have lungs, so they must breathe air through their skin.

Mudpuppies are usually 8 to 13 inches long but can grow up to 19 inches long. They can weigh as much as a pound. Mudpuppies live in the Eastern, the Midwest to the Southern USA. Mudpuppies are fully aquatic, meaning the only place they love is in the water. Mudpuppies have dark red external gills that they use for breathing underwater, just like fish. They hide under rocks and logs during the day and become more active at night. They can even live under the ice when lakes freeze, just like fish do. Mudpuppies eat small aquatic animals like crayfish, snails, insect larvae, and small fish. Mudpuppies can make a grunting sound that sounds like a dog's bark, which is why they are sometimes called waterdogs.

Pacific or California giant salamanders can grow to be 14 inches long. Giant salamanders live in the Pacific Northwest of North America. Giant salamanders prefer clear, cold mountain streams, moist riverside forests, and mountain lakes and ponds. They are one of the biggest salamanders in North America. Giant salamanders can live in water and on land. They are mostly active at night and hide during the day. Some giant salamanders never mature past the aquatic juvenile stage. They can carry a parasite that causes salmonella poisoning in dogs.

Hellbender salamanders can grow up to 29 inches long but are typically around 12 to 15 inches in length. Hellbender salamanders live in the eastern and midwestern USA. They are one of the largest aquatic salamanders in America. Hellbenders have paddle-like tails for swimming. They rely on touch and smell to catch food. Hellbenders have lungs, but they breathe primarily through pores in their skin. They absorb up to 95% of their oxygen through their skin. Hellbenders are carnivorous and eat crayfish, fish, frogs, and invertebrates. Hellbenders are also known as mud cats, devil dogs, snot otters, and lasagna lizards.

Fun Facts About Amphibians

1. Amphibians have very thin, permeable skin that allows water and air to pass through. They can breathe and drink through their skin.

2. Frogs and toads are the same thing. There is no distinction between frogs and toads.

3. Amphibians have survived on the planet for over 360 million years, surviving several mass extinction events along the way.

4. Amphibians have webbed feet that help them swim. The thin layer of skin between their toes helps them push water backward.

5. Frog eggs hatch into tadpoles, which eventually turn into frogs.

6. Amphibians are vertebrates, meaning they have a backbone and an internal skeleton.

7. Amphibians prefer to live in wet environments to keep their skin wet and hydrated.

8. Frogs have excellent night vision. Some male frogs have vocal sacs, which are pouches of skin that fill with air.

Author Page

Billy Grinslott & Kinsey Marie Books

Copyright, All Rights Reserved

ISBN – 9781965098547

Thanks